# Praise for
## *Listening to Mozart*

Following her moving memoir, *Dear Alzheimer's,* about living with
the gradual loss of her husband, Esther Altshul Helfgott's *Listening
to Mozart* is a fitting and lovely companion collection that both takes
the reader through her grieving and celebrates the husband she's lost.
From the new widow's first angry bewilderment *(you must be busy/ —
what are you doing/ that's so important)* to her gradual coming to terms,
she vividly conveys how alive the dead are after they've left us with
their enormous absence.

**—Anne Pitkin**
Author of *Winter Arguments* (Ahadada Books, 2011)


This bouquet of short poems, many in the spirit of tanka, radiates
the sharp and sad fragrance of loss. Esther Altshul Helfgott's words
move in their own breezy yet telling way, reminiscent of Japanese
forms, yet never limiting themselves. These are poems of a deep yet
passing grief.

**—Michael Dylan Welch**
Founder of the Tanka Society of America

Esther writes gracefully and honestly to her husband, Abe. The healing from this loss is ongoing and you experience her continued love, her longing, her pain, along with her acceptance of that loss. You'll grow to love Abe too - their friendship, their marriage, their partnership - as you read the bursts of poetry, short but powerful and sharp.

**—Keri K. Pollock**
   Alzheimer's Association of Western & Central Washington State

Informed by her husband Abe's Alzheimer's disease, Esther Altshul Helfgott's poems share the pain and poignancy of life after his death. *Listening to Mozart* takes the reader on a journey of loss; tragic and beautiful, these poems like miniature portraits capturing the small moments remaining: *you left / I stayed—moon /watches/ both of us— / day doesn't.* Questions, understanding, and the details of how to live without another center this book—*I know you / more / now you're gone*—leaving us with the remarkable realization that relationships don't ever end, they just change form.

**—Kelli Russell Agodon**
   Author of *Hourglass Museum* (White Pine Press, 2014)

Esther Altshul Helfgott uses the melody of daily life—waking, looking in the mirror, eating, going to the library or bookstore—to give the reader the feeling of what it is like to keep going after her husband died of Alzheimer's. In *Listening to Mozart*, using tanka (short songs) and free verse poetry, she gives the reader not just a sense of her husband, but also a sense of what it is like to miss him.
This is a gift.

**—David Rice**
   Editor *Ribbons*, Tanka Society of America Journal

Each poem in *Listening to Mozart* reminds us that grieving is a process unfolding in the simplicity of a given moment. Esther Altshul Helfgott's attentiveness to the details of daily life elevates these short, poignant poems to mindful meditations on memory, ritual, creativity, and healing. It is the transformative nature of art, the act of writing that can sustain us through the process: *I write you / onto the page / how else / to keep you with me...* *Listening to Mozart* is a beautifully constructed memorial reminding us that entire galaxies can be found in the face of a grandchild. Helfgott's own insightful lines encapsulate the power of her collection: *I was just writing / and love came out...*

**—Annette Spaulding-Convy**
Author of *In Broken Latin* (University of Arkansas Press, 2012)

Esther shows us life is as simple as sleeping back to back and as complex as replacing tears with poems. She is our poet of memory and poet of loss of memory. When she describes seeing Abe's handwriting and reaching for her heart we all carry that heart in our hearts.

**—Gary Glazner**
Founder and Executive Director, Alzheimer's Poetry Project and Author of *Dementia Arts: Celebrating Creativity in Elder Care* (Health Professional Press, 2014)

In mimicking the tanka Esther becomes Mozart. She is not just listening. The poems hearken to classical love myths that drive all of us to endure. The Marriage of Figaro or the Magic Flute. The poems are pristine celebrations, happy like a rare wine aged over many years. They aren't adolescent infatuation filled with bubblegum and prom. They are the deepest abiding magical elements of love that drive younger dreams. They are the myths that drive our very existence.

**—Doug Johnson**
Editor of Cave Moon Press

洞月亮

# CAVE MOON PRESS
YAKIMA 中 WASHINGTON

2014

# Listening to Mozart
## *Poems of Alzheimer's*

# Listening to Mozart
## *Poems of Alzheimer's*

Esther Altshul Helfgott

洞月亮
CAVE MOON PRESS
YAKIMA 中 WASHINGTON

ISBN: 9780615980133

for our children

what a stellar life you had Abe—
to know the meaning of the word *thymus*
know what it is   exactly
how it functions in the body—
two lobes of tissue
under the body's heart

# Table of Contents

# Part One

# Pulse

my love
who has gone away
came
in a dream last night—
    he forgot to waken me

when I
awoke this morning
I thought your
funeral was today—
it was three years ago

it took
you eight years to die
all that time
I waited for you
to get better—
why didn't
you—

at Thornton Creek
I saw a cormorant sunning
on a rock—
I looked for you—
you weren't there

standing
at our kitchen window
we could see Mount Rainier—
now new houses block our view

I don't know
what the mountain feels
but we liked watching
it change—clouds came
seasons went

on the countertop—
your Group Health nametag
bus pass    scratch pads
in a basket—still

in our jewelry box—
the pearl necklace you gave me
my engagement ring
our wedding bands

I wish I knew
where you were tonight
I'd visit you
will you send me a message—

last night—despair
covered the pillow
where you once slept—
dream washed
it away

I wish I could find you
in my dreams—
you must be busy
—what are you doing
that's so important

someone
asked me—
do you cry a lot
—no
I say—the
poems
are my tears

it's 10 o'clock
and I'm still in bed
thinking of you
not here
today—
again

I loved
when we slept
back
to
back—
until morning
     came

I still feel
your backrubs
a little
to the left
      that's it—

the dog needs out
reason enough to get up
take a shower
dress—find my way
to the door—go

I want
to visit you—
but I don't know
where you are

my friends help me
get up in the morning—
Lucille Clifton
does too—

I haven't paid
much attention
to my diary
lately—

I don't remember
yesterday—it's the same as today
the only difference is
the planet moved
slightly—

I wonder
which galaxy
you're in
now—
are we still
under the same
moon

you left
I stayed—moon
watches
both of us—
day doesn't

a leaf falls
I watch
you pick it up
you
disappear

# Part Two

# Breath

Anne Carson writes—
a brother's life never ends

nor does a husband's
mine's still near me

everyday he's near me

touch my arm
you feel his

today
I walk in the woods
your voice
is bird song—
you hold my hand

walking
in the
neighborhood
sun
shines
on your absence

you
would have been 85
June 14th—
you died the next day—
tonight
a *yartzheit* candle

Every time
I see your writing
my hand
reaches for my heart—

mountains and hills
of points
and curves—
circles
on a doctor's
prescription
pad—

a scrawl
I never understood

*Abraham I. Schweid*

Your name
is still magic
to me

It represents the power
               of the ages
Abraham, our father
               Isaac, our son
Schweid of the smoke-
               filled chimneys

I saw
grandson Ray
last week
he looks like you—
his mouth   his eyes—
I save
your microscope
for him

I found these jottings on a check deposit slip—

Me—*we waste a lot of time arguing*
Abe—*that's ok*
Me—*why is that ok*
Abe—*because we have time*

some days
I want to
die—
at night
moon beams
change my mind

in the breeze
of today's morning
I'm content—
yesterday's despair
scared me to silence

I went to *shul*
to find our East Coast
neighborhood
it's not there anymore—
I can find god anywhere

when I
look in the mirror
I see you
even our hair is the same—
curly and mussed

tonight—listening
to Mozart—
us—holding hands
snuggling in the movies
watching Amadeus

I see you
around every corner—
as I wait
for the light to change—
your eyes meet mine

we worked well
together—especially
in the kitchen—
I liked when we were
friends

I don't go
to *shul* anymore—
your voice
is missing

I'm in the gazebo
writing—you used to watch me
from the upstairs porch
our rescue dog—Butch
beside you—
you're both gone now

the Greek Restaurant
and Pastry shop—our meeting
place is closing
I've missed us at the table
there—now I'll miss us more

I don't agree
with Bishop in *One Art*—
that loss
is no disaster
she means the opposite—
loss is all disaster

Mozart
and winter time
snow
on the windowpane—
I look for your shoulder

I write you
onto the page
how else
to keep you with me—
memory fades your wrinkles

I buy a new pen—
you slip
from the nib—
I write
us home

I miss
you less
when I write

photo—
leaning into each other
as if we
will continue this way
for eternity

I shouldn't long
for what was or wasn't—
we had our days on earth—
thirty years together
may have been enough

you've become my muse
I've never had a muse

men have them all the time
why haven't I—

did you have to die
for me
to find a muse

the distance
between us   takes my
breath away—

in that pause
is everything—

I'm reading
Flannery O'Connor's
*Prayer Journal*—
I wish I were religious
her intensity relaxes me—

how lucky I
am to have
this chair—
the one you used
to sit in

# Part Three
# Sinew

a woman is
her body of work
her thinking
inside her pen

at least
that's true
for me

I'm forgetting
the Alzheimer's years—
I've gone back to our early days
—you read my work—
all of it—
you knew where
commas went—

at our kitchen table
Joan's talking tanka and writing—
I made a salad
she brought dessert—key lime pie
your favorite

when rain falls
I don't mind—rain
brings your visit—
I liked our walks
in the rain—

Sharon Olds
overwhelms me today—
Annie Dillard's
*Tickets for a Prayer
Wheel* softens

if Dillard is angry
she's angry with god and no one specific
she buries her grief
in dependence on
god of love
god of anger
god who protects
god who—

we never spoke much about god

you didn't want me to
take methotrexate but I had to

now they're giving me Embrel
it cost $1500 a month—

your insurance is still paying off—
I got sick—

now I'm back with the methotrexate
that you said I'd have to take the

rest of my life—you were right
but it's better than psoriasis

crawling all over my body
owning it

I should cook
meals with people
more often—
dinner time is
especially
lonely

in Marie Ponsot's
*Among Women* the poet
wanders sitting still—
that's my kind of wandering—
yours too

I didn't like
living with you
in Bothell—
your other wives
lived there—

it felt strange
being a third
wife—

*three's a charm*
you said—

riding
in your 1965 Mustang
—top down—
ripped leather seats
scratching my thighs

at poetry
readings you'd fall asleep—
poets snored

in a coffee shop
treating myself to
breakfast—
writing without
the dog watching me—

the children
were here
today—
they make me smile—
even the grown ones

housecleaning—
I find your birth certificate
and a $20 bill wrapped in
a bank deposit slip—
off to the bookstore

today
I worked in the archives

I forgot
how much I enjoy

digging into old documents—
manuscripts

nobody looks at anymore
except for a lone

researcher who—from
time to time—stops by

you understood
commitment

Emma and I
returned my library book—
she didn't bark at other dogs
the whole way—

bird nests
on our block
are built—no doubt
—with Emma's hair

I didn't know
I was having fun
until I saw
Facebook
pictures
of me and Emma—
laughing
in the park

your
illness sewed
us
together—now
we are one thread

the knot
between us
cannot be
undone—I know you
more
now you're gone

I no longer
wear a mourner's frock—

but on some days—

like today—the third anniversary
of your death—my heart longs

the way you look at me from the picture frame
your eyes listening as if you were alive again

your nonchalant leaning on the ferry rail
your long hair mussed in the wind

the San Juan Islands we just left
telling me—take this trip again

I didn't know
I was writing love poems
to you Abe—
I was just writing
and love came out

# Acknowledgements

*Listening to Mozart: Poems of Alzheime'rs* was inspired by Jane Hirshfield and Mariko Aratani's *The Ink Dark Moon: Love Poems by Ono no Komachi and Izumi Shikibu, Women of the Ancient Court of Japan* (Vintage, 1990), which I read in preparation for a Jane Hirshfield salon at my home on Saturday July 20, 2013. The poets and friends I sat with in my living room that day and who were the first to hear me read the few poems that grew into *Listening to Mozart* included Lyn Coffin, Rebecca Crichton, Katy Ellis, Carla Gruswald, Ann B. Hursey, Cara Lauer, Carol Levine, Geo Levine, Nikki Nordstrom, Mary Ellen Tally, Ken Tally, Molly Tenenbaum, Ann Teplick, Linda Rowan, Joan Swift and Diane Westergaard.

Some of the work herein was published by *The Far Field: Washington State Poets and Ribbons: Tanka Society of America Journal.*

Special thanks to Kelli Russell Agodon, Lyn Coffin, Katy Ellis, Jackie, Ian and Scott Helfgott, Ann B. Hursey, Douglas P. Johnson, Tanya Johnson, Denise Calvetti Michaels, Alisa Minkina, Ruby Murray, Faye Reitman, David Rice, Wynne Schweid, Ann Spiers, Joan Swift, Ann Teplick, Michael Dylan Welch and Diane Westergaard. Thanks also to Soul Food Books, Redmond, Washington; Arts & Nature Festival, Camp Long, West Seattle; and Writers Read, Columbia City library where some of these poems were first read.

# About the Author

Esther Altshul Helfgott is a nonfiction writer and poet with a PhD in history from the University of Washington. Her work appears in *American Imago: Psychoanalysis and the Human Sciences, The American Psychoanalyst, Beyond Forgetting: Poetry and Prose about Alzheimer's Disease, Blue Lyra Review, Chrysanthemum, DRASH: Northwest Mosaic, Floating Bridge Review, FragLit Journal, HistoryLink, Into the Storm: Journeys with Alzheimer's, Journal of Poetry Therapy, Maggid: A Journal of Jewish Literature, Raven Chronicles, Seattle P.I., Seattle Star,* and elsewhere. She's a longtime literary activist, a 2010 Jack Straw poet, and founder of Seattle's "It's About Time Writer's Reading Series," now in its 24th year. Esther is the author of *The Homeless one: A Poem in Many Voices* (Kota, 2000) and *Dear Alzheimer's: A Caregiver's Diary & Poems* (Cave Moon Press, 2013).

Made in the USA
Charleston, SC
02 May 2014